SPICERACK

Life Flavors

2

Savor

Ginger R. Jones

Editor

Pearline M. Pitts-Holt, M.A.

Copyright Page

SpiceRack

Life Flavors 2 Savor

This is a collection of poems about life.
It poetically discusses life, relationships, and the lessons
I have learned in the first half century of my life.

Written over three decades,
(after my original poem notebook was lost),
it is an honest, revealing and a relatable work,
which was written (like I was raised),
to reach all ages, ethnicities and backgrounds.

You'll laugh. You'll cry. You'll relate. You'll reflect.

Just as a memorable meal is enhanced with spices
from the rack,
enjoy the flow and flavor of these poems and
kick back.

Dedications

Family

Helen B. Hampton, Grandmother

The Late Helen Hampton Jones, Mom
(This Book Cover is Dedicated to You)

Mr. & Mrs. James W. Jones Jr. Father & Stepmother
Cosco E. Jones, Son

The Late Cruzmaria Reese
The Late Alisia Iris Reese Hawthorne
My Big A Team
Anthony, Angelica, Ariana
My Little A Team
Isaiah, Mercedes,
Trinity, Josiah & Angel

My Siblings
Casey, Jewell, J3, Gavin, Loleta, Tatrona & Daphne

RIP Kyle & Billy

My Education Benefactor
Dr. Sarah B. Grant

The Joyner Family
The Trotman Family
The Trower Family
All of my Aunts & Uncles & Cousins
My late Aunt Joe,
Bernard Bowen,
The Late William Bowen Sr. & Sarah Bowen
The Bowen Family

William Bowen, Jr.
Elizabeth Bowen,
Mark Bowen,
Mr. George L. Hampton, Jr.
Ms. Cheryl I. Hampton
Mr. Lawrence Hampton
The Hampton Family
The Jones Family
Mr. & Mrs. George A. Jones
Aunt "Kitty" Sharif
Mr. & Mrs. Richard Trotman

All of my Nieces & Nephews

My CA, DC, GA, NY, NJ, PA, VA & NC, NV Family

Pearline Pitts-Holt
(*My Editor & Lifelong Mentor*)
Eric Pitts & Family
Steve Pitts & Family

Susan K. Scott
Jasmine R. Scott
Christine Austin-Williams & Family

Table of Contents

Faith

Family

Other Life Flavors 2 Savor:

Alone but, Not Alone

Bitter Not Better

How Can I Still Complain?

I fell...and You didn't catch Me

I Like Reading a Face

Trash to Treasure

Sometimes We Get Another Chance to Get It Right

Not in My House!

What's Wrong with the Box?

Who Am I?

Petal to the Metal

My Dream...Come True?

I Pondered...

Don't Tell Me How To Grieve!

Thank You
Booking Information
Additional Dedications
Influences & Inspirations

Faith

Now Faith Is…. (My Hebrews 11:1)

Now Faith is…
The surety of what we hope for
& the certainty of what we do not see,
per Hebrews 11:1.
I need to be specific.
I respect Confucius, New Age, and Islamic belief.
But, I choose Christianity.
God the Father, the Holy Spirit and His Risen Son.
Unsuperglue yourself from yourself,
your crib, your degrees, your accomplishments,
Your bling, your designer gear, your money spent.
Please don't get it twisted and bent.
You're blessed from the prayers you,
your parents and your grandma sent.
Now Faith Is…

As Bishop T.D. Jakes says, "Let me go deeper!"
You were in the world,
doing what you were big & bad enough to do,
safety off, mouth cursing, and guns blazing too.
Who do you think called you in from this world & saved you?
Now Faith Is…

Do you really think you saved yourself?
Do you really think your degrees gave you wealth?
Do you really think diet and exercise guarantees your health?
No joke! Real Talk, the devil is a relentless foe, but with a pit bull
grip,
To THE strong tower I must go,
Now Faith Is…

I don't want this struggle;
I don't want to do dis no mo'.
I just need an easy out, an open door.
I did what I was supposed to do;
I didn't ruin my chances like you,
I didn't run the streets Ginger,
like you and your crew.
So how come you're still blessed G?
I thought your knew!
Now Faith Is...

At the cliff, the bridge,
the top of the ridge,
He splurged, although I selfishly surge,
& lose the urge, to press through my mess.
Still He blesses, I confess,
all the tests, I did not pass.
Didn't think I was going to last,
Living hard, while running fast.
Now Faith Is...

The Trinity, which in today's world
is reduced to obscenity,
but still is my serenity,
I choose the penalty,
The Christian label, thru grace enabled,
some think I'm unstable, but I'm able.
I save money with SD TV & internet, no cable.
Saving because I need something for my children's children,
I need to win,
I know most times He is my only friend.
Alone today,
with my life & future, I can't play.
Now Faith Is...

You ask, why I have faith, it's about right now

I let you know,
God is the source from which all blessings flow.
I believe Jesus is the son of God.
I believe in the Trinity.
The crucifixion, the resurrection, the Three in one.
I also believe I am chosen by Him.
He picked, me up from where I was headed.
He moved me from obscurity
to morality with His infallibility,
He pursued me when mankind ridiculed me;
He schooled me, and I know as I do,
you struggle to let Him consistently rule thee.
Now Faith Is...

Now my faith is real,
I've seen Him move in my life,
I've seen Him save me from the nouns---
the people, places and things,
I've seen Him hide me, shield me
with is anointed, armored wings.
I've seen him make me first,
when I should be last.
I've seen Him, in the next moment,
invalidate my sinful past.
I've seen Him push me past ordinary in this world,
with an immeasurable blast.
I've seen my pockets turned inside out broke,
and he bankrolled them with cash.
Now Faith Is...

Now close your eyes, watch your life's film,
see what God has done for you.
I'll bet if you think about it...
He saved you.
He hid you.
He validated you.

He protected you.
After they rejected you.
He presented you in the presence of your enemies.
He gave you discernment for your frenemies.
As Dr. Jazz says, "There's a Judas at every table."
But, I know my God IS STILL ABLE!
Now Faith Is...

Oh I see you're still cute.
You don't feel my spoken word.
You're still in that box, and there you can stay.
We have to reach the world in every respectable way.
I mean the old ways are still THE foundation,
and Holiness is for every generation.
Don't look at change,
and new ideas with degradation.

Don't make others carry their talents elsewhere,
because their worship expression doesn't get you there,
'Cause it's not about you,
It's about we as the body for Christ do,
Lose your ego, change your attitude,
God's army could use an unselfish you!
Now Faith Is...

We've seen new things,
& they pull your heart strings;
Like travel, communication & technology.
For the bad things, sure there's an apology.
Can we focus on the good that has been found?
Like the digitalization of this poem,
for those who couldn't come to hear this sound,
Or are you too loud, too proud,
need recognition from the crowd?
Can we move onward and forward and take care of God's business?
Or don't you think He's a God of order?

Or it won't go on 'cause you're not involved?
It won't be blessed, your attitude is jacked up, & you're still a mess!
Now faith is...

I believe we are 1 body, different gifts.
So let's work together to truth, not myth.
Can't be any way, but His way.
if it doesn't line up with the Word,
What does the Bible say?
Is He still your potter, are you still His clay?
Or are you doing the selfish thing
& have to always have your way?
Ask yourself, fall back people, fast and pray!
Check yourself, remind yourself,
we is da church to this world,
warrior life on, don't play.
Will you accept Christ and let Him give you what you ain't got?
Oh girl, "I got this!"
"No you don't!"
And you're so stubborn, so you won't,
So let me speak what I know,
and obviously...you don't,
Now Faith is ...

Believing in what you can't see.
Doing things you never done.
Believing in the Trinity, the Three in One.
Leaving this sinful world for Jesus freedom and fun.
Having the genuine smile as His child,
Having him skillfully mold your clay,
Having Him fly under the doctor's radar
Like a Stealth.
and in sickness and on your death bed restore your health.
He is my listening ear; he is the one,
who grants strength, removes doubt and fear.
He is also the one who gives you a swift kick in your rear,

When you act like Him, you ain't got time to hear.
Now Faith Is...

Do you trust Him to be yours?
'cause the world will knock you down on its floor.
Please know with God there is a window
for every closed door.
I don't know about you,
It's He,
That I need to improve me.
And great is your faithfulness unto me
And I believe you are there Lord,
I know when others didn't, you cared Lord,
You have me here Lord, when I didn't think I would be,
You place me front & center
so others can hear how you live in me.

Now I pray,
Let me be consistent,
and repentant, not resistant
To your power, your love
and the peace you give.
The forgiveness you give.
The "Keep Me" you give.
The Protection you give.
The doors you closed.
The windows you open and in all these things,
You have granted me grace and given me wings.
Now Faith Is...

In your heart, has He given you a glimpse of your dream?
Let me ask, does it include Him?
It's ok to be successful,
as long as Him you don't forget,
It's fine to dive into the dream water

with purpose and get wet.
But please don't get high and mighty and comfortably just set.
Because just like He put you up, get cute,
He will bring you down & then what will you do?
When your success hits the ground,
and your ride or die friends can't be found,
He is right where he's been.
He's always around!
Now Faith is...

God can restore you even better than you were;
He did it for me,
He can do it for you ma'am.
He can do it for you sir.
He can make clarity out your life's blur.
He can give you credentials
out of residual potential,
From ghetto to suburban and residential,
From the concept to the eventual,
Creating class from the conventional.
Let Him present you!
Let Him Infringe upon you!
Let Him guide you as He hides you!
Then like the Hope Diamond, you come out with a shine.
Go and get yours, I already have mine.
Grow up, quit complaining & stop the whine.
Can I get another soldier of God's army
to stand with me & in Him find
What Faith Is?

By faith, we understand that the universe
was formed by God's command.
By faith, no rain, Noah believed,
& built the ark with His own Hands.
By faith, Abraham & Sarah had Isaac, their son.
By faith, Abraham starting offering Isaac and thought it was done.

Then there was an offering stuck in the brush,
Now if you have faith, you can't be in a rush.
Any great cook will tell you a good meal takes time,
so let me continue on with this rhyme.
You have a dream you want God to polish and shine.
So will you be selfish and complain and like a child whine.
Or like a sculptor, will you allow Him to chisel your path
as your life's road unwinds?
I get discouraged and I'll bet you do too,
But you gotta get up to get down, to do what you do.
So put on your Ephesians 6 armor on & remember your salvation.
Grace and faith during life's storms
As long as you are still here, you have a chance to use your faith.
Even if you checked into the game,
off the bench late,
He is coming back soon, so be found in Him.
Let's get our acts together and turn from sin.
Then it's the everlasting eternal life you **will** win.
And with open arms He can welcome you…
And claim you…
Rename you…
Sustain you…
Contain you…
And exclaim that to you, you and you too…
Now Faith Is…

The End Piece of Bread

The end piece of bread,
you know the one that most people reject,
I pondered that, as I was making my breakfast one morning.
Why is it rejected?
It's thicker than the other pieces of bread.
Are you thicker than most people are?
What I mean is:
Do you learn from your mistakes?
Do you get knocked down and get back up again, fighting?
Or, do you just sit there and do nothing to bless God,
nothing for others, and even nothing for you?
That thick piece of bread, you know,
the one that few want to deal with, or see the value of.
The one piece that people ignore, pass over,
pull out and then put back,
to get to the next piece of bread that they believe is better.

Have you had people pass over you, ignore you,
to get to what they thought was better than you?
I have.
It sure didn't feel good at the time but,
it didn't kill me so I AM STRONGER!

Have you had people pull out of your life and
then try to come back in your life,
like that end piece?
That's pulled out and put back, because,
initially, they still didn't see your value.
I have.
Well... it's too late for them now.
I forgive them.
God knows who you are, though.
You didn't value the gifts God placed in me.

At times, I was so busy mourning your rejection;
I didn't see my own value either.
Now, armed with, & applying, living with Bible knowledge,
camouflage on, day and night discernment vision fully functional,
I declare to you; I know my value now!
I have been created by God.
Christ died for the forgiveness of my sins.
I am like the end piece of bread, you skipped over.
I am strong!

God allows me to hold not only myself up,
but, empowers me with compassion, to pull you up too.
I don't fall apart like the middle pieces of bread anymore,
instead, like the best French toast seasonings,
I have gained wisdom, when you try to come back for the old me;
I am no longer in the same place.
God has transformed and elevated me into the best piece of French toast.

I AM now, THE... end piece bread.

Family

My Grandma, My Treasure

Proverbs 31 woman all the way.

Showers of blessings, on your special day.

I am grateful every day, for my friend, my grandma.

A sense of humor, you certainly have.

An astute listener, and a distinct laugh.

My grandma, my treasure.

Momie Helen is what we call you,

all grandchildren and extended family too.

Decades of missionary service, tireless and consistent,

No mumbling and complaining, no displays or statements of resentment.

My girlfriend, the golden girl, a true treasure indeed.

When we are in trouble, you hastened to our needs.

Your advice, a wise sage has **NEVER** steered me wrong.

A secret keeper, a great listener of the story,

no matter how long.

The fervent prayer of the righteous woman shall availeth much.

And everyone knows, other than your mother,

if you are sick,

nothing is like her homemade chicken soup

and a Grandma's touch.

She makes you feel welcome,

a cool drink, when it's hot.

A hot, home cooked meal at home.

I am blessed to have Momie Helen,

I never feel alone.

And so we honor you, we give you flowers while you're still here.

To our precious treasure, we love you more.

With each passing year.

Dedicated to My Grandmother Helen B. Hampton

Move Forward

I had my child young, pregnant at 19,

20 when my male blessing came.

I said he wasn't planned,

but he knows I love him just the same.

Now I had him back in the day,

when people would say, Christian, or not,

"You and He won't be anything."

I remember, Denzel Washington so eloquently said,

"Anger motivates me."

So to the tune of overcoming adversity

as a single parent, I began to sing.

My family, my church, my village,

helped me raise my child,

My parenting style, a little old fashioned,

a little in the offbeat file.

Still hearing, the "you won't be anything" song sung in a slow blues style,

I became determined to move both of us forward.

Hustling in the pool room for diaper money

on some called corner shots

Two jobs and school, I worked more than I saw him.

Tuesday night time with him I got.

Tired or not, that Mommy and Son time,

which now, that I am an empty nester,

still means a platinum lot.

He went through elementary school with excellent grades,

from middle to high school he made.

I thought that I would have to send him to his father permanently;

when he tried his best not to behave.

Because we believe in God and are extremely close,

he turned his behavior around,

And landed from a disobedient stint, feet on the ground,

to higher education, scholarship bound.

In college, he began to read more books,

which in the beginning he really could not stand.

As his knowledge expanded he began to enjoy reading,

he knew it was required to work his life plan.

Able to get along with anyone,

his peers voted him Mr. Junior and Mr. Senior, their chosen one.

By now, the ones who didn't believe we would be anything,

had been won over by my son.

Then the challenge came from him

for me to finally return to school.

I couldn't turn your encouragement down,

all good parents know the deal,

When we both graduated again from college in 2009,

the dream we had become real.

Wherever you are in life while you are reading this,

please assess yourself.

Are you moving forward, or are you stagnant,

living on the tale of your last accomplishment's wealth?

God gave us his best, Jesus his son, death on the cross, the ultimate sacrifice.

Like in Habakkuk "Write the Vision", pray for guidance from God,

and then successfully go

with urgency and efficiently utilized time.

Move forward...

exude excellence with this gift called... life.

This poem is dedicated to God,
my son, Mr. Cosco Eric Jones and my beloved A Team,
Anthony F. Reese, Angelica M. Reese,
The Late Alisia Iris Reese Hawthorne
and Ariana Reese Atwell

and every successful single parent in the world.

Special thanks for the song "Moving Forward" as song by Israel Houghton.

This song saved my life, spiritually.

Mr. Houghton, seeing you lead worship at the 2011 Joyce Meyer's
Women's conference
was a lifetime priceless moment for me.
That moment and CeCe Winans opening the conference
with "Alabaster Box".
You just had to be there...
Worship!

When I Looked, They Were There

When a girl is little she may dream, hope and pray,

For the family God, in His Word does say,

Man + Woman = Children, His Way.

While growing up, a girl may desire,

For that one man who will set her heart on fire,

To pray over her, protect her,

and strategically provide for her,

A partner for her team in the game of life.

When I was a little girl, my father,

uncles & cousins were my world.

I was taught never to cry, never to lie,

and always to spy, because people are not truthful

In or outside your family.

People can only try, to truly know and love you.

When my brothers came along,

Jimmy, Casey and Kyle,

If I looked or sounded like I needed anything,

I looked, and they were there.

I would pull up to my Dad's farm,

I rarely opened any doors,

I looked and they were there.

I was hungry one Sunday morning,

I wanted scrambled eggs and bacon,

My father, the immaculate chef,

commenced to cook my breakfast with love

and no complaining

I made a request.

I looked and it was there.

I was sick and on bed rest, I needed groceries;

I looked and my brother Jimmy was there.

I was sick again, my money was low,

My son, who had learned from my Dad,

Uncles and Brother,

Soon grew up to know, that if I looked,

he should be there.

On my brother's Kyle's 19th birthday,

the first birthday after his death,

I was at the farm and I went to get my bag from the car.

And in the pouring down rain, my father came,

Baseball cap, umbrella steady and sure

Consistently the same,

I looked and my father was there.

In my twenties and thirties,

I prayed and often complained.

I wondered where that person for me would be,

If single, I would remain.

Truth be told, I still wonder,

But not as much,

No time for trivial thoughts and such,

Because if God sends that person,

he may come today,

or even tomorrow.

He truly has a tough act to follow.

Because just like my Father in heaven,

my father, uncles, brothers, cousins and son,

Are truly," Nulli Secundus",

which in Latin means second to none.

With them I will always be Number One.

When I looked, they were Always There.

Happy 69th Birthday Daddy,

Love, Ginger

While I Sat on the Ground

While I sat on the ground, one spring day,

it was beautiful, perfect like spring days are.

I saw the church, to my left from afar.

All kinds of flowers and insects,

and an occasional truck or car.

While I sat on the ground.

The day was beautiful, picture perfect it was,

But I was crying, just because,

I was visiting the graves of my baby brother and his best friend.

The ants crawl and the bees buzz.

While I sat on the ground.

It has been almost a year,

and still the memories are crystal clear.

Those memories I cherish, oh so dear,

of our beloved Kyle.

I wanted to talk to you again, if only for a while,

instead of your voice, I heard your smile.

While I sat on the ground.

I heard your smile in the spring breeze,

I saw your smile through the sway of the trees,

And on this flawless day,

I feel God's creations are well pleased.

While I sat on the ground.

Kyle, while I was writing this poem;

Daddy called to check on me,

Not only you and Billy, but Daddy and Diane I came to see,

and writing, and crying, and praying,

I cannot quickly flee,

While I sat on the ground.

Today I sat calmly on the ground,

nearly a year ago, in grief I collapsed.

Today still grieving, I am calm, perhaps,

because, as Jesus, the Lamb of God was pure,

like millions, Kyle made his election sure.

And that assurance is my only palliative cure.

Heaven is where I will see your smile again.

Standing now, this Christian race I run

without phoniness (you hated)

I WILL WIN,

Determined to move forward now,

I am now...

No longer sitting on the ground.

This poem is dedicated to my brother Kyle Jones and his best friend William "Billy" Drake.

To my knowledge, they are the 1st Minority man and Caucasian man to grow up,

die and be buried side by side in Southampton County, VA

(Location of the Nat Turner Revolt)

Thanks for living colorblind brotherhood.

That's what America should be about.

Rest in Peace. We love and miss you.

Special thanks to Erykah Badu for the song "Telephone".

Your voice, the lyrics of this song, and the music,

especially the featured flute,

(My brother Kyle was a southpaw flautist),

continue to assist me in the grieving process.

Other Life Flavors

2

Savor

Alone but not Alone….9/16/08

Today I turned 45, I live alone.

A previous, who texted me to wish me

"Happy Birthday!"

recently broke my heart,

Alone, but still Alive!

An interested neighbor

in my new found aloneness

knocked on the door.

Cards and gift in hand,

I'm still numb from my heartbreak.

Alone, but not Alone.

Got to work and logged in,

Received well wishes from my son, and my best friend,

Text from my sister and yet another text from

Another man interested in me.

Alone, but not Alone.

Well wishes from coworkers on this half day,

It's Mexican Independence Day,

at my job I could not stay,

After all, it was my birthday.

Alone, but not Alone.

Yesterday, my grandmother

lost one of her best friends,

I put my last five dollars in church, but still I win.

In the mail, a card from my beloved "A team"

I'm one they still highly esteem.

Alone, but not Alone.

Stood up for dinner, but with instilled strength,

I treat me.

To dinner I still go.

I see a group of women teachers

who just prayed together.

Didn't they know?

I read my birthday cards in their view.

Outside their group they chose not to pursue.

Alone, but not Alone.

Overcoming heartbreak,

Encouraging music on my car stereo,

As I go home to be alone,

My Jersey Diva Aunts, Kitty and Cordell,

Ring my phone.

Alone, but not Alone.

Alone, we must give and commit our lives to Christ.

Alone means no people, and that has to be alright.

Often times, being alone keeps you walking toward His marvelous light.

The times I felt all alone,

My Lord reminded me,

Alone is how I sometimes feel,

But

With HIM I will NEVER be...alone.

This poem is dedicated to all the ministers who have kept me covered.

I love you!

Bitter Not Better

When people are rude and mean,
When things don't go as well as they seem,
When some darkness overshadows the daylight of your
dream,
It can make you bitter, not better.

When the reason for a person
in your life is just a season,
When your close knit country
has betrayal and treason,
When your healthy body becomes sick,
and falls apart for no reason,
It can make you bitter, not better.

When you thought that deal or promotion was on lock.
When you saved and invested and
a drop happens to your stock.
When someone invades your space criminally
& your safety's off and your gun is cocked,
You are then, bitter, not better.

When you study, and move to application of your religion,
and try to live it,
When you do wrong, and people do you wrong,
and then neither forgive it,
When people act perfect,
instead of leading by example, or living it
You become bitter, not better.

When you look at people,
who you perceive to have it all,
And you can afford the thrift store,
while they shop endlessly at the mall,
When you thought you had
a great relationship, and then,
he or she doesn't even call,
It can make you bitter, not better.

Anger is a real feeling,
an intense emotion.
It usually occurs when there is decrease of devotion.
It is dangerous and moves
like a tsunami on the ocean.
If left not neutralized,
anger can cause harm in an emotional explosion.
All because you are bitter, not better.

I wish I could tell you anger and bitterness
haven't happened to me.
But truthful, a decree that would not be.
I have displayed conduct unbecoming behavior for others
to see.
I've let people "have it"
to the umpteenth power and degree,
because I displayed anger
and lowered my standards to be,
bitter, not better.

I wish I could tell you that from
bad experiences I am all healed.
But I believe in truth, even though it hurts,
I like to keep it real.
I don't really want to be phony,
I want to reveal not conceal,
I have been bitter, not better.

There are wounds I've received,
and, honestly wounds I have given.
There are deep wounds where people have gone in,
ripped out my heart and replaced it,
with a superficial substitute for mankind
where a real love should have been.
I may talk to you about a myriad of subjects,
but I'll never really let you in,
because I'm bitter, not better.

Because of life, I'll admit it, I'm a professional loner.
I don't let people in and don't trust,
I stay in a my zip code and zone...
Ah...
I've been around,
and seen people mirror my guarded behavior,
so I'm a cloner.
Can we just remove the mask,
and to your genuine feelings be an owner?
'Cause, like me, you may be bitter, not better.

Oh! You ascribe to a particular religion,
and you think you are immune.
You are judgmental,
but don't pass your gift off on me too soon.
Because, just like in music,
life's accidentals are coming to your world...
Headphones on, treble up and bass boom,
and please do stay tuned,
Will the Son Shine after your life's darkest moon?
Will life make you bitter...or better?

How Can I Complain?

How can I still complain?

When Christ Died For Me.

How can I still complain?

With the gifts He is entrusting in me.

To sing, play instruments, to write freely

and speak intelligently,

How Can I Complain?

How can I still complain?

When I am blessed to work for others and

To bake cheesecakes without a recipe,

with a gift You gave me.

How can I complain?

How can I still complain?

When I was raised to serve YOU,

I turned the other way, but I knew.

Had my son, people constantly stated to me,

we would never be anything.

To the naysayers who thought we couldn't,

we DID make it!

How can I complain?

How can I complain?

When I see my family and friends

who believe in me, encourage me.

A people that pray first, let God lead the way.

How can I complain?

So if you find yourself complaining about this life,

concerns of misery and strife,

Start to write down your blessings,

you'll smile and stop your stressing.

How Can You Complain?

The truth is, we complain

because we compare ourselves to other people,

times, places and things.

Obedience is better than sacrifice.

Plant a well rooted life garden, let God farm your life's garden

with His sunshine and rain,

and your sorrows will turn to your life's joy from pain.

Then you won't remain the same,

You will embrace your blessings!

Then you won't complain.

I fell... and You didn't catch Me

Place your name in the blank!
We talked & got to know each other for months,
Or at least I thought we met each other in the middle.
If we honestly bared our souls and walked love's plank,
I gave you marquee billing in my life,
I upgraded your friend status & rank,
I fell...and you didn't catch me.

Back in the day, before all this technology,
You could get caught up in what was all too unreal, a fantasy,
You could go on & on for long times of lies and calamity,
Not so today, too much access to evidence, can't say that wasn't me,
Worldwide web, microphone & background check,
search engine there for you to see,
I fell...and you didn't catch me.

I don't want you to think this applies to
just dating relationships,
This can to apply to work and even people
you thought were ride or die friends,
You trusted and made them a VIP, gave them a House Key,
private # access & you're thinking,
they had your six and then disrespect begins
and your season of trusting ends,
I forgive you, thanks for the lifetime lesson,
our season of love & friendship must end,
prayers from my heart to heaven for me & you, I continue to send.
Place your name in this blank;
you know who you are,
This can also apply to me, and who I was, improving, better today by far,
I fell...and you didn't catch me.

Discernment is a skill we must master,
instincts we must always keep in the forefront.
Being nice is one thing, but, in the age of selfies, this is real talk,
Unsuperglue yourself from yourself, being blunt,
You have-
must personify my government name
and proceed Gingerly,
try not in life to get cut,
I fell...and you didn't catch me.

When I was much younger,
and seniority on a job I logged,
I was more than qualified and you think you gave me the job,
As a minority,
I still had to be better that your chosen Bobbie or Bob,
It hurt me when that promotion, didn't happen,
I smiled and continued to feed my family,
even though you knew it was me you robbed,
I fell...and you didn't catch me.

These scars don't heal easily;
these crevices can't easily mend,
I can serve you because I love service genuinely,
but you'll receive my top layer,
The superficial, not the subcutaneous blend,
I learned to become comfortable with me;
my loner status may very well never end,
Because everyone can't earn the title of being my friend,
People are mostly for themselves and work deceitfully,
The only entity who has never forsaken me is God,
His burden is light and his yoke is easy,
Unlike you, He knows all my faults and still loves me,
He turns my bad out for my good,
He listens and shields me from you and even myself,
He provides me something even Gates & Buffett can't do
with their limitless wealth,
He grounds me and provides me, my best true self,
I fell and yes...God caught me.

I Like Reading a Face

I have studied how to read a face.

I like to see when people keep it together with style and grace.

Like my favorite show, "Lie to me", though no expert, I know the basics.

Enough to know if you are true, or, if you are a faking it.

How I wish I had this skill in my twenties,

It would have saved me a lot of pain and heartache.

It is amazing how people think you don't know.

But just like the sun shines, the truth your face will show.

I have learned that people will lie at the drop of a dime,

The swiftness with which they make a lie flow,

Makes a jaguar or cougar running, almost look sublime.

Save yourself some headaches,

Take a basic facial and voice recognition class.

And you will stop wasting time, with people who don't care about you.

Knowing what you see and hear from them,

Allows you to pray for them, and leave them safely.

ALONE!

I like reading a face.

This poem is dedicated to the genius of Dr. Paul Ekman,

The Criminal Justice Department at

Tidewater Community College

And

Retired Assistant Police Chief (Norfolk, VA)-Sharon Chamberlin

and the greatest police department in the world

New York Police Department (NYPD)

Trash to Treasure

I like to shop. What girl does not?

Everyone loves a bargain. You know... shop till you drop.

Designer this, designer that.

When it all comes down, is it really all of that?

One can be beautiful on the outside, and still be no good,

Like a Jag with a detail,

and no ornament on the hood.

We can all do better, in that respect.

We all can observe the things we take for granted,

while holdin' it down 'til our next paycheck.

The air and ability to breathe,

I hate to see people take that for granted.

It's like we roll around like seeds in the air that are not truly planted.

And oh!

Don't get me started

on how we treat other people,

putting them down, judging them, taking them for granted.

We should be living Love and sprinting with purpose to help people.

So in this poem, I wish to say to you today,

Count your blessings;

don't take for granted what's given.

Because your trash,

could truly be another person's heaven.

Sometimes We Get Another Chance To Get It Right

I'm so glad Jesus died for my sins,

Great is Your faithfulness,

proclaims the book of Lamentations.

A new day as a Believer, another chance to get it right.

Why would I try to keep up with the Joneses,

when my last name is already Jones?

Learned my lessons now,

another chance to get it right.

If you ate the wrong thing or didn't exercise today,

It is a new day,

another chance to get it right.

Did you say the wrong thing?

do the wrong thing?

Apologize!

Another chance to get it right.

I practiced my scales on my flute and with my voice,

whew those accidental notes,

I need more practice,

Another chance to get it right.

I'm still learning my way around the Queen City,

and I started the 3rd time, with the same company.

Made mistakes in my twenties and thirties,

Another chance to get it right.

I made the time to make the volleyball games

and help you with your resume',

Even though, my son is grown,

I'm still a parent, still trying to get it right.

Finally, my soul mate feels reciprocity to me,

no one is perfect.

I love God, I love him, and of course,

he gets another chance to get it right.

Everyone makes mistakes, even you the reader.

The question is...

Who will you give another chance to get it right?

Dedicated to all the sinners of the world like me.

Let's learn from our mistakes!

Not in MY House!

I had strict parents, who set house rules,
you had to say "Yes Sir" or "Yes Ma'am" and not cut the fool.
Good grades were expected,
To be brought home from school,
No disobedience in class,
You better not act a fool.
Not in THEIR House!

We had chores to do, and they'd better be done right,
No back talk or mumbling under your breath
In my parent's sight.
Their rules-You were wrong-no discussion-
My parents were right.
Don't even think about putting up a fight!
Not in THEIR House!

I used to visit both grandparents'
& other relatives' house as a child.
Whether up North, when cold,
or down South where the weather is mild.
If I fell out of line, the familiar audio would play,
On repeat, no need to rewind
Not In MY House!

I really don't like profanity,
People with command of any language,
Alternate your vocabulary,
Surely with all your options,
You can either choose silence
Or speak intelligently,
Clutter or disorganization in my house
Will quickly move you from guest to enemy.

This my space,
and if respectful to me and mine you aren't,
Then you can't be,
In My House!

The world outside your door can be SO cruel,
Once outside your door, that's a domain,
You no longer rule,
You can't teach rude
Unaccountable people respect.
They can be stubborn as a mule.
They can't... In MY House!

Does anyone remember
the not too distant past?
When people would respectfully choose the sidewalk,
And not your lawn or grass.
When a fence was optional,
Because family boundaries had already been cast,
Because it was YOUR House.

I'm no expert,
So I can't say today's lack of respect,
Can be attributed to any one thing.
Maybe if people would exude happiness,
And in genuine love, loose their selfish cling.
If they would lose all of the divisions,
And instead harmoniously sing.
NOPE-not happening!
Outside MY House.

My mom taught us your home IS your sanctuary,
your place of peace,
It's where you give and receive love,
and hatred, prejudice and any type of attacks cease,
The world outside will chew you up
And eat you like a beast,

This is your safe place in the world;
It's quiet, accepting and stress free.
That's why it's YOUR House!

When I was little, there were consequences
For your bad behavior on the way home,
I remember if there was any kind of loss
People would call or visit rather than leave you alone.
I remember the world was kinder;
You'd rather help the community and forego your selfish tone.
If you open your door and I open mine,
And step out to help each other,
Then we can build the community zone,
I've been hurt just like you;
Let's meet in the middle of the road with a smile,
Working past our differences
With no audible groan.
Outside OUR House.

What's Wrong with the Box?

What's wrong with the box you put me in?

You said as a single parent of a male child,

I could not win.

You shook your head,

as if you never committed a sin.

What's wrong with the box?

What's wrong with the box racism put me in?

You see my skin color, you eye my hair, my locs,

You even see my gender, again you state I can't win.

What's wrong with the Box?

What's wrong with the Box?

America can sometimes size us up to be.

I am SO gifted, yet you underrate me,

You refuse to see,

still a successful entrepreneur God allows me to be.

What's wrong with the box?

What's wrong with the box?

When an old fashioned girl, born nice

But made defensive by the mean world,

Functioning like a man,

beautiful like a girl.

What's wrong with the box?

The truth is...the box exists.

The mind won't let the heart take risks.

Whatever happens is...

The Creator of ALL gifts,

Gives the gift, to...

Think outside of the box.

Who Am I?

I am the girl doing one arm pushups,

saying put up or shut up.

I'm the multi-ethnic woman who's studied and learned,

Naturally adorned, on the scene.

I expect the best,

I AM the queen.

You, my king, should not settle for nothin' less,

'nuf of life stress,

Let me take my crown off,

lay my locs on your warrior chest and rest.

From our continuum of life and lovemaking,

marriage ordained by God,

which,

my king leaves you breathless.

There is nothing more beautiful to me,

than a real world, everyday extraordinary soldier man.

Except for, maybe you and I dreams shared, resources pooled,

As side by side, we through this life, in perfect

Sympatico teamwork with God stand.

So my lifetime teammate,

let the trivial things of life go,

Praise God from whom ALL blessings flow.

Only HE could bring together,

allow you to find me, and make our friendship lifetime lasting.

OH! OH! OH!

My GOD,

HE'S sweet, I know!

Dedicated to my future Husband.

God knows who he is.

Petal to the Metal

Petal to the metal, if I speak,
I do it with an opinionated mouth.
With family ties originating up north,
but mostly in the south.
I carry multi ethnic background swag,
classy and proud,
I speak in a multi dialect intonation tones,
from soft to medium, not loud.
Petal to the metal

Petal to the metal implies
a mixture of the beauty, softness and strength.
It mixes the strong scent and beauty of a flower,
with the endurance of steel.
It means maybe someone has class and tact
with mass appeal and still...keeps it real,
I think also it can convey the description
of how a woman may sometimes feel.
Petal to the Metal

My life expounds on the petal to the metal concept indeed,
I am a woman,
who now works and continues to succeed,
in a male dominated field, baking and writing,
and wherever my life may lead.
Petal to the Metal

In my job, I have to be twice as good as the guys,
to even be considered good,
My military family members prepared me
mentally & physically until I knew I could.
I mean I have to carry my load,
execute my duties, and not be misunderstood.

I deal with everyone genre of society,
from aristocracy to the hood.
Petal to the Metal

Now, as a multi ethnic individual
that is middle-aged,
I have had to keep my cool when at times,
I indeed was enraged,
I've witnessed violence and racism
of all kinds
that could fill more than book,
chapter and page.
Petal to the Metal

I hail from a family with a proud history
of military service and education.
My family has helped defend the rights of,
secure the freedom & educate this great nation,
It has seen the struggles of Americans from coast to coast,
tragedies, and their frustrations.
Petal to the Metal

Now if you have heard of, seen the plays,
& chick flick movies, you may be thinking,
So far this poem is nowhere close to what I was expecting,
not even an inkling.
Well, categorizations are the predecessors to prejudice,
when diversity smells successful,
it ain't even stinking.
Petal to the Metal

Because my parents gave me world experiences
and didn't raise me in a box,
I like everything from NASCAR to classical music
and Bob Marley with dreadlocks.
I would rather see the content of your character,
than look down the barrel of your gun cocked.
Petal to the Metal

You can see the difference in the world now
in how some people react.
Some have a since of entitlement,
even though the hard work and character they lack.
But some still work on dreams with no real plan,
and hope millions to stack.
I am a loner, an original, and I don't run with a pack.
Petal to the Metal

There is something about being
half a century it seems,
That makes you scrutinize all you've done
and what you dream.
It makes daily life more urgent
and cutting unnecessary persons
from your patterns and seams.
Petal to the Metal

Plays and chick flick movies deal with friends
and the courage to fully be alive.
They expound on sisterhood, family life
and the willingness to thrive.
They deal with living life to its fullest
and in spite of challenges and adversities survive.
Petal to the Metal

I have experienced a life of rich experiences,
great times and on hard times I fell.
Life and love can be wonderful
or sometimes lead you to heartbreak hell.
I've found in life,
discernment and the blindness of love
don't always mix well.
Just because they seem good,
don't always buy everything people sell.
Petal to the Metal

I am a chameleon, multi- faceted
NEVER to be categorized.
If you have a box you've placed me in,
then it is for you I sympathize,
I am a Jackie of many trades,
knowledgeable on trivia,
you... I may surprise.
I am often underestimated based on my gender,
multi ethnic background, and of course,
my size.
Petal to the Metal

We all have put people in a box recently
or during life at some time.
And then been surprised,
when they jump out the box,
and unwrap the twine,
Let's do better world!
And to diverse possibilities,
to truth subscribe and unapologetically unwind,
Is your Petal to the Metal?

This poem is dedicated to:

My Aunt, The Late Sally Brooks
A Retired W.A.C (Women's Army Corps) Veteran

My Step Daughters
SSGT Angelica Reese
SPC Ariana Atwell
United States Army

All Women who have/still serve in the Military
All Women who "hold it down" during Military Deployment
All Women who have/still are employed in Law Enforcement/Security
Thank You For Your Service!

My Dream... Come True?

How do you do...My Dream come true?
I appreciate the polite, "Miss, How do you do?"
Respect more than not, will get you cool points in my book,
Let's see if we can get past, "Hello"... My dream come true.

Let me expound.
"What type of person are you on the inside?"
I need to look into you, past what I can see.
How do you treat people?
Your Family?
Do you respect people consistently, or just initially?
Respect is a foundational attribute that attracts me.
My dream come true.

Do you have a dream,
and a work ethic to back it up?
Do you honor your spiritual foundation?
Or have you given that up?
Much later on ...
if we get past chemistry, will you back me up?
Are you my dream come true?

We all have physical qualities that we like
But do you look good, and your personality bites?
Are you consistently my dream, or just average or okay?
No real person, but just hype.
Love can be blind and I'm too old,
to be wrong and not right,
My dream... come true

I know there is a box, a checklist that is real,
I know there are some things that... if done, will break the deal.
In honesty, will you bear your soul and keep it real?
My dream...come true.

I prayed for,
and for a while my dream has been the same.
It's a constant dream, I am single, but, don't wish to remain.
To be clear, being single for me, doesn't have a banner of shame,
I just want the right, not the wrong person, to light my flame
My dream… come true.

I encourage singles to stay ready
and never stop the dream.
Get your best dish ready,
to sit down to the table with your dream.
Because one of the worst things that could happen is…
To not be
emotionally,
financially,
spiritually & physically ready.
And miss the light beam,
And instead of coming true…
You've missed your dream.

I pondered...
(In memory of Alisia Iris Reese Hawthorne)

Highly unusual,
I woke up in the middle of my evening nap, (I work overnights)
I checked my phone and saw Angelica on my message light.
I knew instantly something wasn't right.
I listened to her voicemail & her voice was unsteady,
but, as usual, polite.
A trained soldier whose voice masked a difficult plight,
Before I dialed her back...I pondered.

I dialed her back and she gave me the news.
Did I hear her correctly, I was just sleep.
Was I dreaming? Or was I confused?
Alisia had transitioned, passed on, resting...
Her body and soul finally... at peace.
No more needles, no more tubes
Resting like her Mom & Uncles & family
who transitioned before her.
Tears & Screaming, I sat dazed,
I could not grasp, I could not diffuse
Before I dialed Eric... I pondered.

I sat, then I stood... helpless, until Eric arrived
Composure, I am trained to have,
But in grief, I hollered, I screamed while I cried.
I missed her already and that could not be denied.
Until Eric arrived,
which wasn't long, but seemed like forever,
myself I was beside...I pondered.

So young, but yet a magnolia of steel.
One of my favorite memories of Alisia Is as a little girl,
Running around in purple socks,
Screaming like her favorite cartoon, "I can do anything!",
and as an adult, living what she screamed as little girl...for real.

Fighting diabetes and instilling fight in her girls.
Finishing at the top of her college class
Though her circumstances and health weren't ideal,
these things...I pondered

The last time we spoke at great length, we talked about a visit to ATL
"I would like to Ginger, as soon as I'm feeling well"
We exchanged, "I loved you" with no regrets,
We were genuine, Alisia was a sweet spirited person,
she wasn't a hard sell.
Don't ever waste an opportunity to be genuine with those you love.
Sure in this life, with people there will be differences,
don't let them continue on for a spell.
Let pettiness loose!
Life is here today, gone tomorrow.
Let the good priceless memories prevail.
As I cried...I pondered.

Alisia's favorite color is purple, the color of royalty,
And she was a princess, not only in the classroom,
Just like in the eye the Iris, (Alisia's middle name)
provides color and light for all of us to see.
She loved with all her heart
Mercedes, Trinity and Angel & all her friends and family.
Now, so big a hole in our lives and hearts,
as through this, we process and grieve.
We can hardly breathe; through tears we can hardly see.
I have some questions God...
like her Mom & Uncles and other family members before her,
Also gone... just like Alisia soo young.
With us why among us can't they be?
As I sighed...I pondered.

I'm a writer, and for days and weeks,
since your transition, Alisia,
I prayed for the right words to come.
Then in a group text to the remaining A team
(Anthony, Angelica & Ariana) and Eric (He's the +1),

Ariana didn't reply to the group, just to me, alone, not everyone.
She gave me THE verb, the title for what we're doing,
Our physics graduate provided the simple sum,
She responded via text,
when my words to express my feelings were gone.
A writer, still words I had none.
Ariana replied..." I'm Pondering"

So I continued to wait for the words after all, I had a deadline,
I'd promised Andre, Deidre, and myself,
that the paperback would be done.
The finished product should reflect Alisia's radiance,
it should reflect our teddy bear one.
Her life and my words must exude her life and align.
I am not a procrastinator.
Grieving gave me writers block, I was running out of time.
I am meticulous about my work
and can't put just anything together like some,
But one week to go, and still not all at one time,
as usual, still the words had not come.
After no sleep, after working all night.
Finally, the words did come.
I no longer have to ponder.

I no longer have to ponder.
I no longer have to wonder.
God is supreme, He's superlative!
Death is never man's place to make a call,
We are hurting now, were sensitive.
I have to...we have to continue to work.
We are all family Created by God, woven together by Alisia.
Look to your left to your right, we have a mission, we are all now relatives.
Everyone who hears or reads this,
Know This!
Death teaches us how precious life is to live!
You are probably thinking, Alisia is not here to speak to,
so what more can I give?
Look at the legacy she left in her daughters,
a testament to motherhood.

Perseverance, Real Fight,
Great Sense of Humor, (those funny faces).
All Truth and Alisia was real.
She was no fib.
Promise (if you haven't already,)
to work together to make sure her daughters know,
that family unity, instilling heritage along with love & faith,
is the path that we must continue on and go.
Resolve to be available, to love and guide always, and to
Mercedes, Trinity & Angel show,
We are here for you.
We are here for each other.
Alisia we miss and love you so!
Think that as you leave this service.
Recite to be love and let love flow.
Live life, be available to those you love.
Learn from life as you wander to and fro.
Enjoy those you love and from your smile,
be light and radiance...from the inside out... glow.
Rip the runway of life.
Praise, dust shake, go and then...flow.
Love & family are the things we should grasp daily and not ponder.
These are the things Alisia passed with her purple baton.
These ideals are our bonder.

This family needs you, and will continue to need you!
Make room on your calendar.
Be Available!
Lend your love and time.
This is urgent.
We're counting on you to be a consistent responder.
How can you be there?
What time and talents to this family can you offer?
Smile when you call back
Lend us your best you and, don't you dare be somber.
The greatest leader is a servant first.
These are the things we should all ponder.

Don't Tell Me How To Grieve!

I just lost someone that I love.
I am going through.
I know you want help me.
Be careful with what you say,
how you treat me.
Proceed Gingerly.
Ask!
Don't make assumptions,
unless you know me.
Please don't tell me how to grieve!

According to the Kubler-Ross Model, and,
depending on which of the five stages I am in:
1. Denial
2. Anger
3. Bargaining
4. Depression
5. Acceptance
Grief changes my sane,
when it enters life's game.

Everyone processes grief differently.
Some people work through it for sanity.
Some people call friends endlessly.
Some people weep & holler in a frenzy.
Some people isolate and process quietly.

What works for you may not for me.
It makes us different, you see.
So I ask you respectfully,
let me handle it, in the way that's best for me.
The one thing that is always appropriate
during loss to genuinely say,
Is...
"I am sorry for your loss."
Don't say anything else,
'cause you don't know how I feel,
even if our losses our similar.
I implore you & my case I appeal.
Please don't say I am weak,
because I shed tears,
and still shed tears.
You don't know the magnitude of my loss.
As a Christian, I believe Jesus died on the cross.
And He was God's only Son, He paid my sin cost.
True to me it is,
it still,
right now doesn't sooth my heart's loss.
Don't Tell Me How to Grieve!

There are losses of some people in this life,
that will knock the wind from your sail.
And only in getting up
and moving past your grief will living life prevail.

When loss occurs,
those who care and want to help you.
Find something for them to do...
so they can help you and feel useful too.
Help, that if you allow it,
will move you past your sadness and pride,
and concede.
Loss is handled differently,
because people aren't the same.
It's a fact to accept and believe.
You may think you have the answers after my loss,
But I implore you respectfully,
Please keep them to yourself,
This loss is mine,
and hurts me more than your heart
and mind can conceive,
Please don't tell me how to grieve!

Thanks!

I hope you enjoyed your

poetic snack from the SpiceRack.

New ideas for poems

are being penned by me, regularly.

In Volume II of this series,

it won't be another ½ century,

through rhyme, before I say, what I have to say.

(Smile)

Press on into your purposeful dream.

There is only one you.

The world is waiting on you to do what you're gifted to do.

Blessings to you and yours,

Ginger

For Bookings

spicepoet@gmail.com

Follow me on Periscope & Twitter

GingerJ@spicepoet

See you in print

Or

At the Mike Check (1, 2-1, and 2)

Or on the other side of life.

More Dedications

Every Co-Worker on each job I worked that encouraged me
_____ (Fill in Your Name) Thank You!!!

FAITH from those I've had the honor of meeting:

Nigel "Legin" Anderson
Joshua Alexander
Rodney Allen
Minister Linda Baker
Dr. Clifford & First Girlfriend Waltrina Barnett
Dr. Jerome Barber
Mr. & Mrs. Jack Bell
The Late Walt "Bells" Bellamy
Eric Blake
The Brown Family
Dr. Roland Carter
Sharon Chamberlin - Former Assistant Police Chief, Norfolk, VA
Dr. Samuel Chand
Corey & JoAnn Rosario Condrey
Reverends Reginald & Evelyn Davis
The Dix Family
Melvina Dorn
Darlene Dorsey
Samuel Dorsey
Mr. Lloyd & Dr. Donna Elliott
The Epps Family
Dr. Emory Fears
The Fernandez Family
Connie & Jarrett Fountain
Rev. Jack & Mildred Gaines
Juan Garedo & the Late Vanessa Garedo
Bishop B.J. (Bring Jesus) & Evangelist Gatlin

Cindy Gray
Mrs. June Green
Minister Gilda Harris
Dr. Michael and Rev. Twanna Henderson
Rev. Laquinnya Henderson
Dr. Debora Hooper
Charles & Valerie Hunter
The Late Cedric R. Hunter & the Hunter Family
Rev. Leon & Rev. Dr. Sandi Hutchinson
Eddie & Priscilla Jackson
Rev. Brenda Jones
The Kerns Family

Ms. Evelyn Keys
(My Beloved Voice Coach &Music Mother for 30+ years)

Brenda (Sylkie Smooth) Livermon
Rev. Jawwad & First Lady Tammi & Lexi & Elisha Love
The McNeal Family
Marchia Mickens
Adrian & Lena Mungo
Rev. Solomon Missouri
Vernetta Nichols & Roberta Downing-
(The Best Seamstresses this side of Heaven)
Ike Owens
Vince Preister
Stacey Tyler
Minister Susie Stevens
& the New Beginnings Community Church Choir-
Accompanied by the tightest church band on this planet.
(I love & miss you)
The Reese Family
Minister Willette Robinson
The Late Dr. Georgia A. Ryder
Rev. Gavin & Mrs. Angie Wainwright
Rev & Mrs. Milton Williams

Mr. Cosco Williams
Dr. Anthony & the Late Sherry Witherspoon

The A.M.E. Zion Church
Brighton Rock A.M.E. Zion Church-Portsmouth, VA
Faith A.M.E. Zion Church-Atlanta, GA
Gift of Life Church-Virginia Beach, VA
Midtown Bridge Church, Atlanta, GA
The United Methodist Church
St. Mark United Methodist Church-Atlanta, GA
New Beginnings Community Church-Matthews, NC

Special Thanks to the Poet &
Spoken Word Artist Communities
Of the Following Cities:

Atlanta
Charlotte
Las Vegas
Los Angeles
London, United Kingdom
Minneapolis/St. Paul
Newark
New Orleans
New York City
Philadelphia
Sydney, Australia

And

Eternal Thanks
To My Foundational Fans
In
The
(757), (804)
And The

FAITH from those I have yet to meet:

Bishop T.D & First Lady Serita Jakes
Bishop Hezekiah Walker
Bishop KW & Elder Valerie Brown
Bishop B. Courtney & Janeen McBath
Bishop Orrin & Dr. Medina Pullings
Christian Broadcasting Network (CBN)
Toure' Roberts & Sarah Jakes Roberts
Dr. Marvin Sapp
Dr. Jasmin Sculark
Kevin Bond
Nick & Christine Caine
Dr. Thema Bryant-Davis
Kirk & Tammi Franklin
Fred Hammond
Mr. & Mrs. Israel Houghton
Michael & Gail Hyatt
Dave & Joyce Meyer
Pastors Joby and Sheryl Brady
Pastor Jentezen and Cherise Franklin
Pastor Steven and Holly Furtick
Prince Hadley
Pastors Larry & Tiz Huch
Pastors Steve & Sharon Kelly
Lecrae
Pastor & Mrs. Van Moody
Sophia A. Nelson, Esquire
Pastor Smokie Norful
Pastor Paula White
Pastors Joel & Victoria Osteen
Pastors Benny & Wendy Perez
Dr. James and Mrs. Betty Robinson
LaChina Robinson
Pastor Marcus and Joni Lamb

Pastor Kim Burrell
The Clark Sisters
Tasha Cobbs
Pastors Rick & Kay Warren
The Hawkins Family
The Winans
Vickie Yohe

Other Influences & Inspirations

The Late Arthur Ashe
The Late Langston Hughes
The Late Dr. Maya Angelou
Nikki Giovanni
Sonia Sanchez
Kathleen Battle
Jonathan Butler
Jessye Norman

Mrs. Evelyn Wall
(My High School English Teacher)

Jon Goode
(VA in the House)
Poet Noble
(NOLA in the House)

All Poets in the Bowen Family
Karen Briggs

Missy Elliott
*(Same Hometown & High school
but I'm older than you, smile)*

Quincy Jones

Jennifer Hudson
Al Jarreau
Debbie Allen
Phylicia Rashad
Earth, Wind & Fire
Roberta Flack
Rachelle Ferrell
India Arie
Common
Queen Latifah
Jill Scott
Jonathan Butler
The Late Donny Hathaway
Lalah Hathaway
Bobbi Humphrey
The Late Phyllis Hyman
The Late Whitney Houston
Bruce Hornsby

The Late B. B. King
(*My Birthday Buddy*)

Bonnie Raitt
James Taylor
Carole King
Bob James
Nathan East
Earl Klugh
Anita Baker
Michael Franks
The Late Bob Marley
Ledisi
Melba Moore
MC Lyte
Rick Fox
Cheryl Miller
Cynthia Cooper

The Late Kim Perrot
Gina Prince-Bythewood
Steve Harvey

Shanaan Dawda, CPA
Suze Orman
Dave Ramsey

The Late Barbara Jordan

The Marsalis Family
(Jazz NOLA)

Mindi Abair
Angella Christie
Jessy J
Pamela Williams

Dr. Mehmet Oz
Dr. Donna Roberts & Staff
The Late Tito Puente
Troy Polamalu
Tyler Perry
Robin Roberts
Sonya & Dell Curry
B. Smith & Dan Gasby
The Crew on ABC's The Chew

Patrice *(Baby fingers to the 10th musical power)* Rushen

Sheila E.
Gloria & Emilio Estefan
The Late Max Robinson
Randall Robinson
Willi Smith
Esperanza Spalding
Kirk Whalum
Tatiana Whitlock

Oprah Winfrey

Stevie Wonder

SpiceRack Life Flavors 2 Savor 2 is already being written.

Thanks for your prayers & purchase.

Leave this world better than you found it!

www.ingramcontent.com/pod-product-compliance
Lightning Source LLC
Chambersburg PA
CBHW060415050426
42449CB00009B/1978